SECRET STARS

James Muirden

CONTENTS

STARRY, STARRY NIGHT
Galileo and Stars
3

STAR PICTURES
Constellations
6

GUIDED BY THE LIGHT
Navigation
8

SPACE FAKES
Comets and Meteors
10

A STAR IS BORN
Nebulas and Planets
12

DWARFS AND GIANTS
Star brightness
14

DOUBLE DAZZLERS
Binary stars and Gravity
16

THE MILKY WAY
Galaxies
18

OUT WITH A BANG
Star death and Supernovas
21

INDEX
Quiz answers
24

WALKER BOOKS
AND SUBSIDIARIES
LONDON • BOSTON • SYDNEY

1 Galileo Galilei was born in 1564 in a town called Pisa, in northern Italy. He grew up to make important discoveries about the things we see in the night sky.

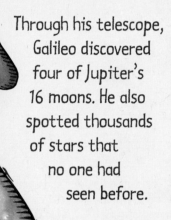

2 No one knows who actually invented the telescope, but in 1609 Galileo found out that a Dutchman named Hans Lippershey had made one. Galileo then had the bright idea of using one to look into space.

3 Through his telescope, Galileo discovered four of Jupiter's 16 moons. He also spotted thousands of stars that no one had seen before.

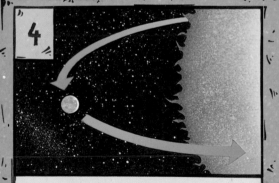

4 What really caused a stir was when Galileo claimed that the Earth travelled around the Sun. In those days nearly everyone else believed it was the other way round — that the Sun travelled around the Earth.

5 Galileo's ideas were thought so dangerous that he was locked in his home to stop him from spreading them. This didn't stop Galileo carrying on his work, though, and he continued studying and writing about space until his death in 1642.

2 GALILEO

STARRY, STARRY NIGHT

1 Have you ever tried to count the stars? On dark nights you can see hundreds. There are lots more you can't see, though, because they're so faint they can only be found using a telescope.

2 Astronomers are people who study the stars. They think there may be a hundred million million million altogether — that's 100,000,000,000,000,000,000,000!

3 Stars look tiny from Earth. But if you could visit one, this is the sort of thing you'd find …

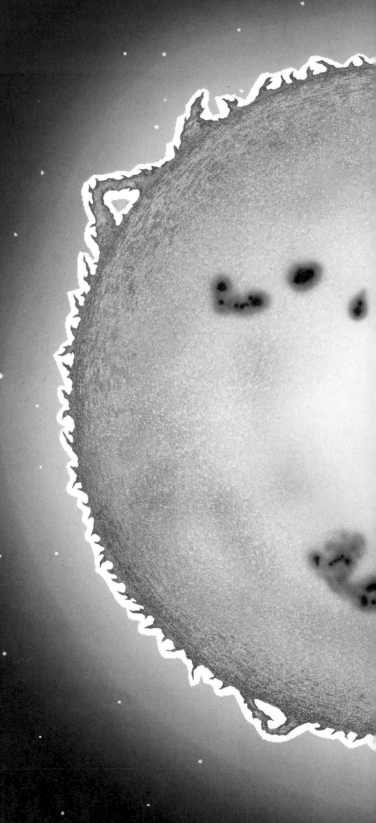

4 ...a vast, scorching-hot ball of glowing gas — much like our Sun, because the Sun is actually our nearest star!

5 The Sun may be a close neighbour, but it's still 150 million kilometres away from us. It would take about 150 years to travel that far in a car!

6 We'd all be frizzled if the Sun was any nearer though, because it gives out as much heat as 1,000 million million million million electric fires all switched on at once. Temperatures at the centre of the Sun are about 15 million °C.

4 STARS

7 The Sun is dazzlingly bright, too. You should NEVER look directly at it, in fact, because its light is so strong it could harm your eyes, even on hazy days.

8 Even so, the Sun isn't particularly hot or bright compared with other stars. And although a million Earths could fit inside it, it isn't all that big either.

9 Some of those tiny twinkling lights you see on starry nights are gigantic — big enough for a million stars like our Sun to fit inside them!

STAR PICTURES

1 Meet Orion, the hunter. He's a constellation, a group of stars that make a picture — if you join them up like a dot-to-dot drawing and use a lot of imagination!

2 We don't know who first drew constellations, but we do know it was happening 5,000 years ago in the area we now call the Middle East.

3 Back in ancient times, people made up stories to explain where the stars came from.

4 Orion was first drawn by the Ancient Greeks. In their stories he was a giant who could walk on water.

6 CONSTELLATIONS

5 The Greeks believed that after Orion died, their gods put him in the sky, where he's fighting a constellation called Taurus, the bull.

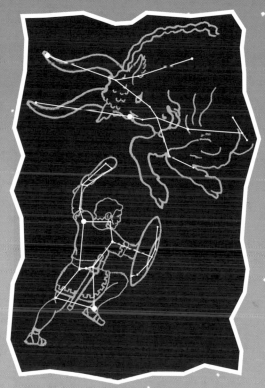

6 Picking out a constellation is never easy. You won't be able to see Orion every night, but he is one of the clearest — look out for the three bright stars that make up his belt.

1 Throughout history, people the world over have looked at the stars and seen different patterns.

2 Orion was named by the Ancient Greeks nearly 3,000 years ago. About 1,000 years before this, the Ancient Egyptians had looked at the same stars and seen Osiris, their god of the dead.

3 The Moche people lived in South America more than 1,400 years ago. To them, the three stars in Orion's belt showed a thief being attacked by giant birds as a punishment.

4 And around 200 years ago, the Pawnee Indians gazed into the night sky above the plains of North America, to see three deer running and leaping through the darkness.

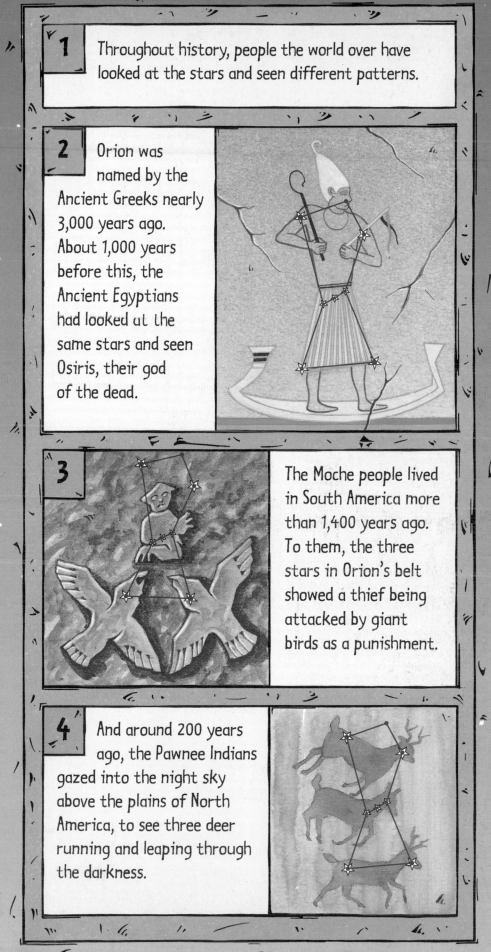

GUIDED BY THE LIGHT

1 Navigating means keeping track of where you are and in which direction you're going, so it's very important when you're travelling.

2 For thousands of years, travellers have used the constellations as signposts to help them navigate.

3 Two constellations are particularly useful, because they help us to find the north and the south.

8 NAVIGATION

4 The Little Bear constellation points towards the north, while the Southern Cross constellation is used to find the south.

5 Each constellation is a bit like a compass in the sky, since if you know where north or south is, you can work out other directions, too.

1 You can't see all the constellations at once — just those in the sky above where you're standing. That's why travellers in the northern and southern hemispheres navigate by different stars.

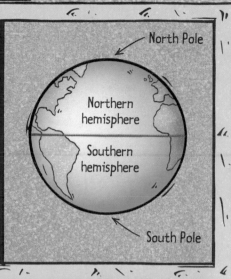

North Pole

Northern hemisphere

Southern hemisphere

South Pole

2 In the southern hemisphere, if you look at the midpoint between the Southern Cross constellation and the bright star Achernar, you're facing south.

Southern Cross

midpoint

Achernar

3 In the northern hemisphere, the Pole Star points the way north. It's the star at the tip of the Little Bear constellation.

Pole Star

Little Bear

4 Nowadays space satellites are used to send signals to help ship and aircraft pilots find their way. Even so, when pilots learn to navigate, they're still shown how to use the stars — just in case their modern instruments break down!

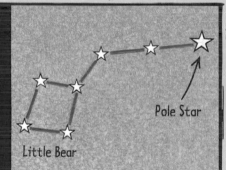

SPACE FAKES

1 From time to time a strange "star" shines in the night sky, only to disappear a few weeks later. It's not really a star, of course, it's a comet.

2 Real stars are made from gas. But comets are mountain-sized lumps of snow and dust — more like gigantic dirty snowballs than stars!

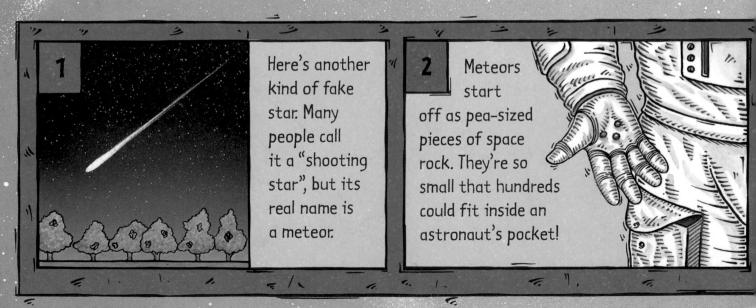

1 Here's another kind of fake star. Many people call it a "shooting star", but its real name is a meteor.

2 Meteors start off as pea-sized pieces of space rock. They're so small that hundreds could fit inside an astronaut's pocket!

3 Comets are space travellers that journey round and round our star, the Sun. At times they're very close to the Sun, but at others they're millions of kilometres away.

4 Comets may look bright, but unlike stars they don't make their own light. We can only see comets when they come close enough to the Sun for its light to shine on them.

5 When a comet does get close to the Sun, its snow becomes boiling hot and turns into a gassy cloud. This streams out behind the hurtling comet and is called its tail.

3 When pieces of space rock hurtle through the air around the Earth, they burn up and vanish. From the ground they look like bright lights streaking across the night sky, and these flashes of light are what we call meteors.

4 Some people believe that you should make a wish if you spot a shooting star. But it'll be gone in a flash, so you'll have to be quick!

A STAR IS BORN

1 Did you know that the stars you see in the night sky weren't always there, and that a new star is born somewhere in space every year?

2 Stars begin their lives inside a nebula — a vast, dark cloud of dust and gas.

3 Every now and then, big clumps of dust and gas start whirling around inside the nebula, spinning faster all the time.

4 Astronomers call these clumps protostars, which means "not-yet-stars". Over time, a single nebula may give birth to thousands of them.

5 As each protostar spins, its dust and gas are pulled inwards into a ball. The protostar gets hotter, too, until it begins to glow.

6 Slowly the protostar grows hotter and brighter — until one night, millions of years later, a newborn star is sparkling and twinkling in the sky.

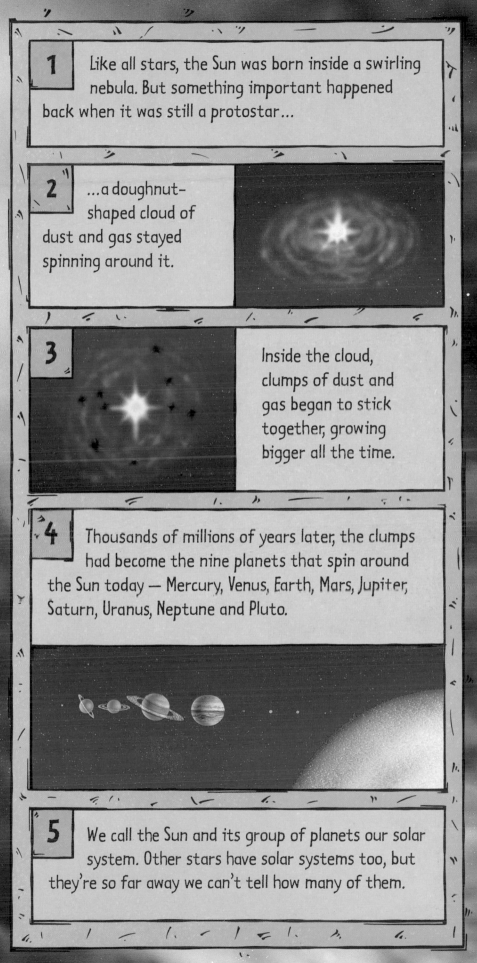

1 Like all stars, the Sun was born inside a swirling nebula. But something important happened back when it was still a protostar...

2 ...a doughnut-shaped cloud of dust and gas stayed spinning around it.

3 Inside the cloud, clumps of dust and gas began to stick together, growing bigger all the time.

4 Thousands of millions of years later, the clumps had become the nine planets that spin around the Sun today — Mercury, Venus, Earth, Mars, Jupiter, Saturn, Uranus, Neptune and Pluto.

5 We call the Sun and its group of planets our solar system. Other stars have solar systems too, but they're so far away we can't tell how many of them.

1 Imagining the different brightnesses of stars is difficult, but one helpful way is to compare them with lights on Earth.

2 A medium-sized star like the Sun gives off a strong yellow-white light. Think of it shining like the bright electric bulb in a desk lamp.

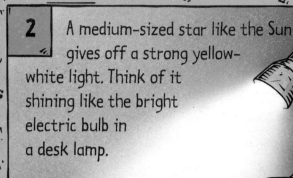

3

If the Sun shines like a desk lamp, a red dwarf's faint ruby glow is no stronger than the light given off by the standby button on a television set.

4 But blue giants are so huge and hot that they beam out like a lighthouse, putting every other star in the shade!

14 STAR BRIGHTNESS

1 Most stars look fairly alike from Earth, but if you could travel out to them you'd see they come in different sizes, and shine with different colours and brightnesses, too.

2 The smallest and dimmest stars are called dwarfs. The largest and brightest are called giants. And in between there are medium-sized stars like the Sun.

DWARFS AND GIANTS

3 Red dwarfs glimmer faintly with a dull reddish glow. They reach temperatures of 3,000 °C — which may sound like a lot, but is cool for a star.

4 Medium-sized stars like our Sun are about ten times the diameter, or width, of a red dwarf. They're twice as hot, too, and their starshine is yellow and bright.

5 Blue giants are the real superstars, though! At up to ten times the diameter of the Sun, they glare out 100,000 times more fiercely, with a dazzling bluish-white light.

STAR BRIGHTNESS 15

DOUBLE DAZZLERS

1 New stars are born together in big families called clusters. Then as they get older, most of them drift away to shine on their own.

2 But about a quarter of all stars are born as twins and stay together all their lives. They're called binary stars — "bi" means two, as in the word bicycle.

3 Everything in space travels around its own invisible pathway called an orbit. The Moon travels around the Earth, for example, while the Earth travels around the Sun.

1 What is the pulling force we call gravity like? We can't see it, but we'd know if it wasn't there. Without the Earth's gravity tugging downwards, everything would float off into space like lost balloons.

Binary stars spend their whole lives travelling around each other. This is because each star's pulling force — its gravity — is strong enough to keep them together.

5 Some binary stars are very close and orbit each other in hours. But others are so far apart that a single orbit can take thousands of years!

2

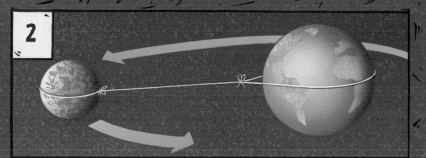

It's the Earth's gravity that holds the Moon in orbit around us, too. It's like an invisible piece of string stopping the Moon from flying away.

3 Everything in space has gravity. The more massive it is, the stronger its gravity. The Sun is so much more massive than the Earth that its gravity is powerful enough to keep all nine planets and their moons orbiting around it.

THE MILKY WAY

1 All the stars you see at night are just a tiny part of a vast starry grouping called a galaxy.

2 There are lots of galaxies in space. We call ours the Milky Way, and this is what it looks like from above. Our Sun is just a dot about a third of the way in from the edge.

3 Astronomers think there are at least 200 billion stars in the Milky Way. But don't start counting them — it would take you well over 60,000 years!

4 Like everything else in space, the Milky Way is swirling round and round. It isn't moving very quickly, though.

5 The whole thing turns so slowly that it has only spun round once since the first dinosaurs lived on Earth, 220 million years ago!

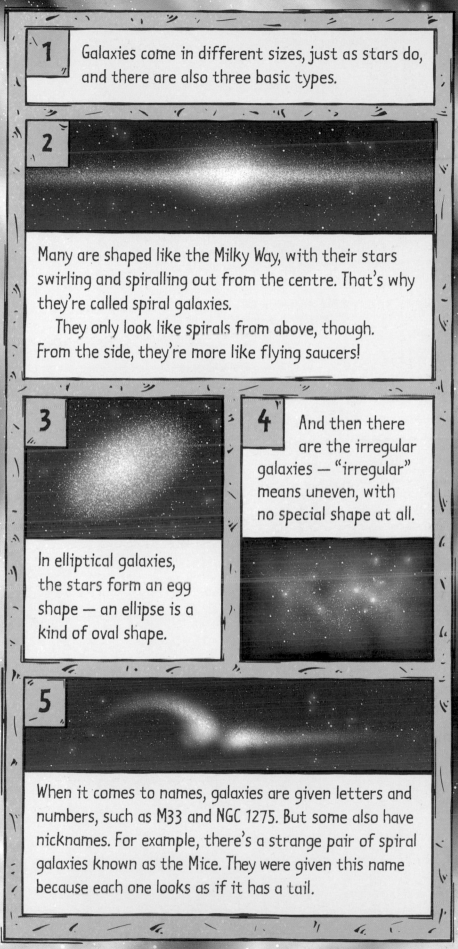

1 Galaxies come in different sizes, just as stars do, and there are also three basic types.

2 Many are shaped like the Milky Way, with their stars swirling and spiralling out from the centre. That's why they're called spiral galaxies.
They only look like spirals from above, though. From the side, they're more like flying saucers!

3 In elliptical galaxies, the stars form an egg shape — an ellipse is a kind of oval shape.

4 And then there are the irregular galaxies — "irregular" means uneven, with no special shape at all.

5 When it comes to names, galaxies are given letters and numbers, such as M33 and NGC 1275. But some also have nicknames. For example, there's a strange pair of spiral galaxies known as the Mice. They were given this name because each one looks as if it has a tail.

1  Our Sun is a middle-aged, medium-sized star. It's been shining steadily for almost 5,000 million years, and there are another 5,000 million years to go before it starts to die.

2 Then, slowly but surely, the Sun will puff up and grow hotter and hotter. The Earth will roast in the heat. The icecaps will melt, and the rivers and oceans will boil away.

3 But the Sun will keep on swelling until it becomes a kind of star called a red giant. It will be about 100 times bigger than it is today, and 1,000 times as bright. It will bake the Earth to a cinder.

4 Hundreds of millions of years will pass, and most of the Sun's gases will float away leaving a speck of brilliant white light — a white dwarf star, about the size of the Earth.

5  The white dwarf will be very hot to begin with, but it will slowly cool down. Within a few more million years the Sun will be a dim speck, and without its warmth the Earth will be frozen and dead.

OUT WITH A BANG

1 Nothing lasts for ever, not even a star. But just as stars look different from one another, so their endings are different, too.

2 A blue giant, for example, only shines for a few million years before starting to die.

3 Then it starts to overheat, puffing up like a balloon until it grows into an enormous kind of star called a red supergiant.

4 The supergiant goes on getting hotter and hotter and hotter, until...

BANG

5 The supergiant blows up like an immense bomb, hurling gas and dust out into space at speeds of around 10,000 kilometres a second!

22 SUPERNOVAS

8 When the light at last fades away, something strange is left behind — a solid ball, only a few kilometres wide.

6 The exploding star is called a supernova, and it's the most spectacular light show in space.

9 It's called a neutron star. It doesn't shine, but it's scorching hot and unbelievably heavy. A piece the size of a grain of rice would weigh 100,000 tonnes, as much as a fully laden supertanker ship.

7 It's as blinding as a billion Suns. And although the blast is over within seconds, the supernova blazes away for weeks — or even months.

10 Astronomers haven't seen a supernova in our galaxy for nearly 400 years, but they believe that one explodes somewhere in space every day. So who knows, you could be lucky enough to see one tomorrow!

INDEX

A

astronomer 3

B

binary star 16-17
blue giant star 14, 15, 21

C

cluster, star 16
comet 10-11
constellation 6-9

E

Earth 2, 16, 17, 20

G

galaxy 18-19
Galileo 2
gravity 16-17

L

Little Bear 9

M

meteor 10-11
Milky Way, the 18-19
moons 2, 16, 17

N

navigation 8-9
nebula 12-13
neutron star 23

O

orbit 16, 17
Orion 6-7

P

planet 13, 17
Pole Star 9
protostar 12, 13

R

red dwarf star 14, 15
red giant star 20
red supergiant star 21, 22

S

shooting star, see meteor
Southern Cross 9
Sun 2, 4-5, 11, 13, 14, 15, 17, 18, 20
supernova 23

T

telescope 2, 3

W

white dwarf star 20

Main illustrations by Christian Hook (6); Lawrie Taylor (3);
Ian Thompson (cover, title page, 4-5, 10-19, 21-23); Peter Visscher (8-9).
Inset and picture strip illustrations by Ian Thompson.
With thanks to Bernard Thornton Artists and Claire Llewellyn.
Designed by Matthew Lilly and Tiffany Leeson; edited by Paul Harrison.
Consultant: Carole Stott
First published 1998 by Walker Books Ltd, 87 Vauxhall Walk, London SE11 5HJ
2 4 6 8 10 9 7 5 3 1
Text © 1998 James Muirden
Illustrations © 1998 Walker Books Ltd
This book was typeset in Kosmik.
Printed in Hong Kong
British Library Cataloguing in Publication Data
A catalogue record for this book is available from the British Library.
ISBN 0-7445-2896-8 (Hardback)
ISBN 0-7445-6090-X (Paperback)

QUIZ ANSWERS

Page 2 — FALSE

The centre of a star is the hottest part. The surface temperature of the Sun reaches about 6,000 °C, for example, but at the centre the temperature can be 15,000,000 °C.

Page 6 — FALSE

There are 88 constellations now, but there used to be many more. In 1922, an international committee of astronomers agreed there were too many, and cut the list down to the present number.

Page 8 — TRUE

Scientists believe that some birds, such as blackcaps, use the stars to guide them when they fly south, away from the cold northern winters.

Page 11 — TRUE

Meteor showers are quite common. Most are caused by pieces of space dust given off by passing comets.

Page 12 — FALSE

Some scientists think that only about a quarter of all stars have planets.

Page 15 — TRUE

Some astronomers believe that just over a third of all stars are red dwarfs.

Page 17 — FALSE

Very often, one of the binary stars is much brighter than the other.

Page 18 — FALSE

Astronomers believe that the Milky Way is one of the biggest galaxies in space.

Page 20 — TRUE

The gas from a dying star floats away, and eventually forms a nebula cloud.